My
Passion Project

A Reflective Journal for Finding Fulfillment in Life

Lynn Sheets

INTRODUCTION

We often pour our energy into our work, so much so that it can be mistakenly confused with identity. But what you do for work may not be your "life's work." What you do regularly may not regularly feel meaningful or fulfilling. What you do becomes a habit more than a conscious choice—one formed by spending so much time doing something without periodically pausing to ask: "Does this reflect who I am? Is this what I want?"

Does this sound familiar?

This workbook will encourage you to dive deeper within yourself, to find and follow what makes you feel happy and fulfilled. It is the companion workbook for "The Passion Project: Your Quick and Practical Guide to Finding Fulfilment in Life."

The exercises encourage real-time self-reflection. Be flexible and use whichever resonate most with you. While the exercises need not be completed in order, they are organized in roughly the order I found my direction. You may find that a different order is more useful in your life. Regardless of which way you work through some or all of this workbook, there is no right answer. Do what helps you most.

Most of all, enjoy your journey!

CHAPTER 2: Pursuit of Passion

Exercise: **When Have You Experienced Flow?** (Pg 32)

When have I felt completely absorbed in what I was doing yet things felt effortless and highly enjoyable?

_____

_____

_____

_____

_____

_____

_____

_____

_____

_____

_____

_____

_____

CHAPTER 3: What's Your Identity?

Exercise: **What's Your Identity?** (Pg 40)

I consider my identity to be:

_____

_____

_____

_____

_____

_____

I value:

_____

_____

_____

_____

My themes:

1. _____
   _____

2. _____
   _____

3. _____
   _____

4. _____
   _____

5. _____
   _____

6. _____
   _____

7. _____
   _____

CHAPTER 4: Identity Formation

Exercise: **Identity Status** (Pg 44)

Are you in the career you want for your life?

_____

_____

_____

_____

_____

_____

How did you decide on your career?

_____

_____

_____

_____

_____

_____

What quadrant of the *Identity Statuses* would you classify yourself for your occupation?

_____

_____

_____

_____

_____

_____

Are you living your life according to what's most important to you?

_____

_____

_____

_____

_____

_____

What influenced you in deciding how you want to live your life?

_____

_____

_____

_____

_____

_____

What quadrant of the *Identity Statuses* would you classify yourself for your lifestyle?

_____

_____

_____

_____

_____

_____

Exercise: **Admiration** (Pg 47)

Who do I admire?

_____

_____

_____

_____

_____

What do I admire about them? (What do they do? What character strengths do they exhibit?)

_____

_____

_____

_____

_____

_____

How does what they do or who they are align with what I want to embody?

_____

_____

_____

_____

_____

_____

Whose work resonates most with me (my identity)?

_____

_____

_____

_____

_____

_____

What makes their life's work so appealing to me?

_____

_____

_____

_____

_____

_____

What activities or work might carry that same appeal
and excite me?

_____

_____

_____

_____

_____

_____

_____

Part III: What Do You Want?

Exercise: **What Do I Want?** (Pg 50)

What do I want?

_____

_____

_____

_____

_____

_____

_____

_____

_____

_____

_____

_____

_____

_____

CHAPTER 5: Reflect

Exercise: **Personality Centered Approach** (Pg 54)

Consider how your tendencies make you gravitate toward certain interests. Complete these sentences:

I value _____

_____

I feel happy when _____

_____

I am proud of my ability to _____

_____

How would you summarize what you gravitate toward?

_____

_____

_____

_____

_____

Problem/Solutions-Centered Approach (Pg 55)

Use these questions to analyze what concerns you most in life:

What questions or real-world problems keep me up at night?

_____

_____

_____

_____

_____

What organizations' missions resonate with me most?

_____

_____

_____

_____

_____

What gives my heart the biggest lift?

_____

_____

_____

_____

_____

How would you summarize what you want to focus on?

_____

_____

_____

_____

_____

_____

_____

_____

Interest-Centered Approach (Pg 56)

What would I keep doing if I were a billionaire?

_____

_____

_____

_____

What would I start doing if I were a billionaire?

_____

_____

_____

_____

If I was asked to start an organization, what would it do?

_____

_____

_____

What types of stories or experiences stay with me?

_____

_____

_____

_____

What do I like to talk about?

_____

_____

_____

_____

What content do I engage with the most?

_____

_____

_____

_____

How would you summarize what you're most interested in?

_____

_____

_____

_____

Remembrance Approach (Pg 57)

Picture yourself at age five.

Where do you shine?

_____

_____

_____

_____

What do you love to do in your playtime? (What do you care deeply about?)

_____

_____

_____

_____

What do you love about yourself at this age?

_____

_____

_____

_____

Repeat, picturing yourself at age 18.

Where do you shine?

_____

_____

_____

_____

What do you love to do in your playtime? (What do you care deeply about?)

_____

_____

_____

_____

What do you love about yourself at this age?

_____

_____

_____

_____

Repeat, picturing yourself at your current age.

Where do you shine?

_____

_____

_____

_____

What do you love to do in your playtime? (What do you care deeply about?)

_____

_____

_____

_____

What do you love about yourself at this age?

_____

_____

_____

_____

Think about yourself today.

What do you enjoy doing most in your free time now?

_____

_____

_____

_____

What are you yearning for now?

_____

_____

_____

_____

What interests (personal or professional) support what you yearn for?

_____

_____

_____

_____

Life Experience Approach (Pg 58)

How have my experiences influenced what's important to me?

_____

_____

_____

_____

What do I want in my work? What's ingrained in me?

_____

_____

_____

_____

What wouldn't I change about my work today?

_____

_____

_____

_____

What puts me in a state of flow where I'm so absorbed
that I forget about time or time flies by?

_____

_____

_____

_____

Where do those closest to me (those I respect most and who know me best) see me thriving and most content?

_____

_____

_____

_____

Vision-Centered Approach (Pg 59)

Sketch or jot down your:

Full-time dream work (ignore pay)

_____

_____

_____

_____

<u>Sketch</u>

Retirement dream (what you see yourself doing without a paycheck)

_____

_____

_____

_____

Sketch

What are you enjoying in each sketch? Who and what are you surrounding yourself with? (People? Animals? Machines? Computers? Microscopes? Art? Storefronts?)

_____

_____

_____

_____

What did you learn about yourself from this approach?

_____

_____

_____

_____

Wrap-up (Pg 60)

What were your most illuminating questions?

_____

_____

_____

_____

What did you learn about what you want?

_____

_____

_____

_____

How does what you learned align with your themes from Part II (*What's your identity?* exercise)?

_____

_____

_____

_____

_____

_____

CHAPTER 6: Imagine

Exercise: **Passion Finder** (Pg 64)

Take a positive moment and savor it.

What were you doing?

_____

How do you remember feeling?

_____

Who or what were you interacting with?

_____

Why do you think you felt the way you did?

I felt _____

when I _____

because I _____

Repeat these steps for other moments in your life.

What were you doing?

_____

How do you remember feeling?

_____

Who or what were you interacting with?

_____

Why do you think you felt the way you did?

I felt _____

when I _____

because I _____

Now think about all of the moments that came to mind.

What do they have in common?

I am most content when _____

_____

_____

What activities or roles might allow for more moments like these?

_____

_____

_____

_____

_____

_____

What surprises you?

_____

_____

_____

_____

_____

_____

Exercise: **World Stage Exercise** (Pg 65)

What are you excited to talk about? What do you most
want to share?

_____

_____

_____

_____

_____

_____

Exercise: **Refine** (Pg 67)

What interests stand out, giving you the biggest "lift"
thinking about?

_____

_____

_____

_____

_____

_____

How do your interests align with your identity? With
your values?

_____

_____

_____

_____

_____

_____

_____

_____

_____

CHAPTER 7: Your *It*

Exercise: **Ident-*it*-y Tree** (Pg 72)

Start your first branches by asking either "What interests me most?" or "Who (or what) do I want to help?" Using your results from the Refine exercise (chapter 6), customize the layers of your tree with options that reflect the interests uncovered in Part III (What Do You Want?).

Next, start at the top of the tree and choose the option that reflects what you want to do at each level of the tree. Follow the branch of the option you select down to the next decision point until you reach the bottom.

Exercise: **Visual Litmus** (Pg 75)

Visualize doing the passion you selected today, in this very moment, and fill in the blanks:

I see myself _____

and I feel _____

I see myself _____

and I feel _____

I see myself _____

and I feel _____

I see myself _____

and I feel _____

I see myself _____

and I feel _____

Visualize how you'd feel doing what you selected six months or a year from now and fill in the blanks:

This has impacted my quality of life by _____

_____

and I am feeling _____

_____

This has impacted my quality of life by _____

_____

and I am feeling _____

_____

This has impacted my quality of life by _____

_____

and I am feeling _____

_____

CHAPTER 8: Revisiting What You Want to Do

Exercise: **Finding Disconnects** (Pg 79)

What do I desire for my life?

_____

_____

_____

_____

_____

_____

Is there a difference between what you say you desire and what you identified in the earlier Ident-it-y exercise? If there is, consider why.

_____

_____

_____

_____

_____

_____

Exercise: **Revis*it*** (Pg 82)

Write down what *it* is that you've decided you want to do.

_____

_____

_____

_____

_____

_____

What's changed from what you wrote down at the beginning of this chapter?

_____

_____

CHAPTER 9: Goal-Setting Foundations

Exercise: **Identifying Gaps and Needs** (Pg 88)

What's going well today that you don't want to give up (met needs)? How might you incorporate this into your goals?

_____

_____

_____

_____

_____

_____

_____

_____

_____

_____

_____

What's missing—what don't you have today (gaps)?
How might you incorporate this into your goals?

_____

_____

_____

_____

_____

_____

_____

_____

_____

_____

_____

_____

_____

_____

Exercise: **The Matrix** (Pg 89)

Using the results from the *Identifying Gaps and Needs* exercise, complete the matrix.

I do ...	I like ...
	Professional
	Personal
	Keep it up

	I don't like …
	Professional
I do …	**Personal**
	Stop

I like ...

Professional

I don't do ...   Personal

Get started

	I don't like ...
	Professional
I don't do ...	**Personal**
	Keep it that way

56

CHAPTER 11: Drafting Goals

Exercise: **Roughing Out Goals** (Pg 101)

I want to …

_____

_____

_____

I will _____

so I can_____

I will _____

so I can_____

I need to…

_____

_____

_____

Exercise: **Success Visualization** (Pg 104)

What do you want to do to feel more fulfilled?

_____

_____

_____

_____

_____

_____

What does success look like one month from now?

_____

_____

_____

_____

_____

_____

What actions have you taken to get this far?

_____

_____

_____

_____

_____

_____

What does success look like six months from now?

_____

_____

_____

_____

_____

_____

What actions have you taken to get this far?

_____

_____

_____

_____

_____

_____

What does success look like when you've reached your goal?

_____

_____

_____

_____

_____

_____

What does success feel like?

_____

_____

_____

_____

_____

_____

What actions have you taken to get this far?

_____

_____

_____

_____

_____

_____

What additional actions or goals did this exercise help you identify?

_____

_____

_____

_____

_____

_____

_____

_____

_____

_____

_____

_____

_____

_____

_____

Exercise: **Drafting Goals** (Pg 105)

Think of one or two things you can do now to start pursuing your passion.

_____

_____

_____

_____

_____

_____

Draft two or more goals using the SMART format (Chapter 10), which will start you on what it is that you want to do to live a more fulfilled life.

1._____

_____

2._____

_____

3._____

_____

CHAPTER 12: Keeping Motivated

Exercise: **Grounding** (Pg 108)

Goal Setting	Reflection	Impact
What would I want to accomplish if I had only one year left to live?	*Why is this important to me? How will it make my life more meaningful or grow my contentment?*	*How important is this goal to growing my contentment?*
1.		
2.		
3.		
4.		
5.		

Exercise: **Finish Line Visualization** (Pg 110)

I see myself...

_____

_____

_____

_____

_____

_____

_____

_____

_____

_____

_____

_____

_____

_____

Exercise: **Check-In** (Pg 112)

Am I enjoying this?

_____

Is this how I want to be spending my time right now?

_____

What emotions am I feeling?

_____

_____

_____

What bodily sensations am I feeling?

_____

_____

_____

_____

Congratulations
on the work you've done!

Now it's about staying the course to pursue the goals you designed—goals that facilitate greater fulfillment and enable you to pursue your passion. While this is your journey, we can't accomplish the most meaningful things in life alone. As you tackle your goals, remember the tips for keeping motivated—form a community of support and draw on each other for strength. Last but not least, stay honest with yourself.

Trust in who you are and believe in what you want to be. Your life is your journey. Your honest self is your true self and offers guided direction for your journey. It's up to you to choose the direction you go and what to be in your time. Your honest self provides a natural means of choosing how you spend the time in your life, informing you on which paths to follow and which trails to blaze. Your honest self reminds you: you have your own life to live with unique and valuable gifts to give.

You have the tools and the ability, so enjoy the journey ahead.